Unknown Friends

ALSO BY CARL DENNIS

POETRY

A House of My Own
Climbing Down
Signs and Wonders
The Near World
The Outskirts of Troy
Meetings with Time
Ranking the Wishes
Practical Gods
New and Selected Poems 1974–2004

PROSE

Poetry as Persuasion

Unknown Friends

Carl Dennis

PENGUIN POETS

PENGUIN BOOKS
Published by the Penguin Group
Penguin Group (USA) Inc.,
375 Hudson Street, New York, New York 10014, U.S.A.
Penguin Group (Canada), 90 Eglinton Avenue East, Suite 700, Toronto,
Ontario, Canada M4P 2Y3
(a division of Pearson Penguin Canada Inc.)
Penguin Books Ltd, 80 Strand, London WC2R 0RL, England
Penguin Ireland, 25 St Stephen's Green, Dublin 2, Ireland
(a division of Penguin Books Ltd)
Penguin Group (Australia), 250 Camberwell Road, Camberwell, Victoria 3124, Australia
(a division of Pearson Australia Group Pty Ltd)
Penguin Books India Pvt Ltd, 11 Community Centre, Panchsheel Park,
 New Delhi–110 017, India
Penguin Group (NZ), 67 Apollo Drive, Mairangi Bay,
Auckland 1311, New Zealand
(a division of Pearson New Zealand Ltd.)
Penguin Books (South Africa) (Pty) Ltd, 24 Sturdee Avenue, Rosebank,
Johannesburg 2196, South Africa

Penguin Books Ltd, Registered Offices:
80 Strand, London WC2R 0RL, England

First published in Penguin Books 2007

10   9   8   7   6   5   4   3   2   1

Page ix constitutes an extension of this copyright page.

LIBRARY OF CONGRESS CATALOGING IN PUBLICATION DATA
Dennis, Carl.
Unknown friends / Carl Dennis.
p. cm.—(Penguin poets).
ISBN 978-0-14-303875-7
I. Title.
PS3554.E535U55 2007
811'.54—dc22 2006050716

Printed in the United States of America
Set in Adobe Caslon
Designed by Sabrina Bowers

For Martin Pops

Acknowledgments

Thanks are due to the editors of the following magazines, in which some of these poems first appeared:

The Cincinnati Review ("To Duty" and "String Quartet")
The Kenyon Review ("Our Generation" and "A Visit to West Point")
The Nation ("At the Border")
Night Sun ("The Triumph of Time")
Parthenon West Review ("The God of Dogs" and "With Horses")
Poetry ("Birthday," "Not a God," and "A Teacher Looks Back")
Salmagundi ("Grass," "A Hundred Years," "At the Oak Street Restaurant," "Remorse," and "Report from Eden")
Smartish Pace ("Diary")
TriQuarterly ("Unsent Letter from the Owner of 51 Summer Street")

I would also like to thank the Yaddo Corporation for sponsoring stays at Saratoga.

Finally, I would like to thank the generous friends who gave me valuable criticism on all these poems: Charles Altieri, Thomas Centolella, Alan Feldman, Mark Halliday, Tony Hoagland, and Martin Pops.

Contents

Unknown Friends

String Quartet

Art and life, I wouldn't want to confuse them.
But it's hard to hear this quartet
Without comparing it to a conversation
Of the quiet kind, where no one tries to outtalk
The other participants, where each is eager instead
To share in the task of moving the theme along
From the opening statement to the final bar.

A conversation that isn't likely to flourish
When sales technicians come trolling for customers,
Office-holders for votes, preachers for converts.
Many good people among such talkers,
But none engaged like the voices of the quartet
In resisting the plots time hatches to make them unequal,
To set them at odds, to pull them asunder.

I love the movement where the cello is occupied
With repeating a single phrase while the others
Strike out on their own, three separate journeys
That seem to suggest each prefers, after all,
The pain and pleasure of playing solo. But no.
Each near the end swerves back to the path
Their friend has been plodding, and he receives them
As if he never once suspected their loyalty.

Would I be moved if I thought the music
Belonged to a world remote from this one,
If it didn't seem instead to be making the point
That conversation like this is available
At moments sufficiently free and self-forgetful?

And at other moments, maybe there's still a chance
To participate in the silence of listeners
Who are glad for what they manage to bring to the music
And for what they manage to take away.

Diary

All that's kept me so far, I want to believe,
From reading the diary of a friend
Sent me last month by her niece as a memento
Is the fear of intruding on moments of self-communion
She didn't intend to share. Even in death
Her right to privacy ought to be respected.

Just that scruple, with a little extra support
From the fear of finding, in her vivid phrasing,
An all-too-candid assessment of my character.
When I'm ready for candor, even the harsher passages
Will seem like letters of rare sincerity
Sent from beyond the grave for my instruction.

As for any pages suggesting my friend
Judged the town I've considered ample
Confining, that she dreamed of a circle
Freer in spirit than ours, more questioning,
Even that discovery would seem worth making
To someone whose love of the truth is genuine.

For a pilgrim spirit, just knowing more clearly
How little one knows is a big step forward,
Just knowing how many miles
Friends may stand from each other
Even when they stand close, brimming over
With fellow feeling, and almost touching.

Meanwhile, here is her thick blue book
Unread on the shelf by my desk, waiting

For me to reach out. It won't be long now,
I want to assure it, before my wish for the truth
Overcomes all resistance, or my fear of the truth
Is overcome by my need for company.

At the Border

At the border between the past and the future
No sign on a post warns that your passport
Won't let you return to your native land
As a citizen, just as a tourist
Who won't be allowed to fraternize with the locals.

No guard steps out of a booth to explain
You can't bring gifts back, however modest,
Can't even pass a note to a few friends
That suggests what worries of theirs are misguided,
What expectations too ambitious.

Are you sure you're ready to leave,
To cross the bridge that begins
Under a clear sky and ends in fog?
But look, you've started across already
And it's one-lane wide, with no room for U-turns.

No time even to pause as drivers behind you
Lean on their horns, those who've convinced themselves
Their home awaits them on the other side.

With Horses

The life of spirit that some have found
In meditation or self-forgetful service
She's found in the quiet company
Of those guileless, graceful creatures.

Too bad that her schedule, crowded
With seven lessons, two feedings, mucking five stalls,
Leaves her only a slender margin for friendship.
It hurts her to phone from the stable to say
She's running late again, that her would-be friend
Ought to see the movie he promised to see with her
With someone else.

No one more deliberate and more thorough
In teaching the fundamentals and the finer points
Of a practice nearly as old as poetry.
And then the lesson she gives without trying,
The particular joy that blooms
Only in the company of another species.

It's true that the kind of riding she loves, dressage,
Looked unnatural in its movements
When I first observed it, but so did ballet.
Not a race to the finish line and the winner's circle
But the art of going nowhere in style
As the two in motion sign to each other
With gestures too subtle for me to catch.

Ten years of training at least, like learning a language
Or a private dialect with just two speakers.

Not for her the illusion she'll find another speaker,
Once Ollie's joints begin to vex him,
Without another decade of practice.
This is what she gets, she knows, for choosing
An art that limits itself to a mortal medium.

I get some comfort from hoping
Some of my words will get on without me.
But I wouldn't claim it's as vivid as what she feels
On a walk in the pasture, after her chores are done,
When old, rheumatic Casper, retired years back,
Comes hobbling up to nuzzle her shoulder
And be nuzzled in turn. He may not know
What's happened to him exactly, but he knows
She doesn't hold it against him and hasn't forgotten
What the two of them shared with no one else.

Unsent Letter from the Owner of 51 Summer Street

Now that you've lived for a month
In your new house at 52 Summer,
I thought it might do you good to know
Why you still haven't met me,
Your neighbor across the street,
And why, if I can prevent it, you never will.

I'd like to begin with the solemn promise
The developer made me that nothing
Would ever be built on the spot
Your house now fills completely.
Nothing was to block my view of the hills
That made me feel my life, constricted till then
For reasons I'd rather not go into,
Was open at last to possibility.

I want you to try to imagine the year
I found in the hills my inspiration,
And then the following year I wasted in court
In a vain effort to stop construction.
To listen to all the details so you understand
How deeply your presence wounds me,
Though of course I don't expect you
To put your house on the market and vanish.

I simply want you to realize that your house
Figures in darker plots than the plot of a comedy
Where luck steps forward to solve a housing problem.

I'd like my letter to serve as a cloud
Passing over your house on a sunny day
Long enough to remind you that across the street
It's raining, and somehow you're partly responsible.

Yes, a larger person, writing such words
To vent his disgruntlement, might decide in the end
Not to send them, the wish to protect and pardon
Stronger than the wish to jolt the unknowing.
But try to imagine me as a man
With little interest in being large.

If I hesitate, it won't be a sign
I want to spare you. Only a sign
I don't believe you'll care to listen. No,
You'll shake my words off, I predict, as surely
As I might shake off words equally carping
If I had as little experience of the world
As you are likely to suffer from
And as little interest in gaining more.

Boys at Play

Tomorrow they'll be a blur, the three black boys
I passed this afternoon at play in the school yard
A block from my neighborhood. But this evening
It seems they're enough to lift from the dark,
By a single thread, three I'd forgotten,
Who crossed the street in the factory district
Of downtown St. Louis to play with my brother and me
One afternoon fifty years ago.

It must have been summer, '49 or '50,
One of those Saturdays when Dad brought us along
When he drove in to scan the mail for orders.
Nobody on the street as my brother and I
Played in front of the office, and suddenly
Three boys our own age, ten or eleven,
Crossing over to us from behind the junkyard.

Three slender black boys looking a little raggedy,
Half-smiling, uncertain but curious, and eager,
It seemed to me then, if I remember rightly,
To get acquainted. All three with nicknames,
I think, though I can't recall them;
And one showed us the toy he'd made,
A squarish plank with roller skates nailed to the bottom,
A kind of proto-skateboard cobbled from street junk
That he urged us to try, though we were wary.

Amazing how much comes back, though who can say
If I'm forgetting what's most important.
They must have lived in one of the two apartment buildings,

Civil-War vintage, still inhabited when the area was rezoned
For factories like my father's. Both torn down
A few years later, the residents scattered.

The boys would be men of sixty now, if alive.
If not, it's likely they weren't done in
By the kind of rare disease of the nerves
That did in my brother, his muscles weakening
Till even breathing became impossible,
But by something predictable, the daily strain, say,
Of a job where personal style meant nothing.

Maybe I'm being unfair to assume
They couldn't escape statistics with a little luck
Or some extra determination.
Even back then they may have stood out
In their readiness to play with children
As strange as we must have seemed.

An afternoon of laughter and friendly shouting
In a game of street tag they may have recalled
With feelings not cordial once they surmised,
If they hadn't guessed already,
How many choices would be denied them.
Still, when I call them to mind, they seem strangely free.

I remember our play concluded
With a friendly exchange of gifts
Like those that Homer's heroes might have engaged in

If they happened to meet on the road and discovered
Their parents had hosted each other decades before.

This bowl, this shield, this bag of marbles, this cap gun,
Exchanged among us before the shades of the prison-house
Closed over us, as Wordsworth says in a poem
That forgets to draw the distinction
Between the child lost in the dark
And the child that's father of the man.

Our Generation

Whatever they'll say about our delinquencies,
They'll have to agree we managed to bridge the gap
Between those who arrived before us
And those who followed. We learned enough
At the schools available to fill the entry-level positions
At the extant sawmills our elders managed,
At banks, drugstores, freight yards, and hospitals,
Then worked our way up to positions of trust.
There we were, down on the shop floor
Or up in the manager's office, or outside the office
On scaffolds, washing the windows.
Did we work with joy? With no less joy
Than people felt in the generations before us.
And on weekends and weekday evenings
We did our best to pursue the happiness
Our founders encouraged us to pursue,
And with equal gusto. Whatever they'll say about us,
They'll have to agree we filled the concert halls,
Movie houses, malls, and late-night restaurants.
We took our bows on stage or waited on tables
Or manned the refreshment booths to earn a little extra
For the things we wanted, the very things
Pursued by the generations before us
And likely to be pursued by generations to come:
Children and lawns and cars and beach towels.
And now and then we stood back to admire
The colorful spectacle, the endless variety,
As others before us admired it, and then returned
To fill our picnic baskets, drive to the park,
And use the baseball diamonds just as their makers

Intended they should be used. And if we too
Crowded into the squares to cheer the officials
Who proclaimed our country as fine in fact
As it is in theory, as faithful a friend to the planet
As any country we cared to name,
A few of us, confined to a side street,
Carried signs presenting a view less fanciful.
A few unheeded, to be sure, but no more unheeded
Than a similar few in generations before us
Who hoped that in subsequent generations
A message like theirs, though no more pleasing,
Would be more welcome.

Smaller

Though our city is only half as populous
As it used to be, it still may suit you
If you don't require a long line at the bakery
To convince you the bread's authentic.
Try to be glad there's room now
At the Himalayan Center, on its busiest evening,
Not only for you and your mat
But for any student who comes in late.
No crowding as you practice the breathing
That calms the soul, that frees it
To drift among your concerns without attachment.

With the noise from the street only half as loud
As it used to be, you can hear, as you chant,
The hum from the church next door
As the AA regulars in the basement
Steady the shaky resolve of a new member
Or confirm their own. Here's your chance
To consider the mystery of unfair allotments:
Why the moderation easy for the disposition
That you were born with is a lifelong
Struggle for dispositions like theirs.

The subject may be addressed in the sanctuary
A floor above them this very Sunday.
With attendance at services down by half,
Whoever stands in the pulpit may conclude
A gospel of fellowship isn't likely to triumph
Without some help from denominations
Beyond the usual range of an outreach program,

Those that are ready to widen
Their own definitions of "ecumenical."

And what if that wider circle includes even you,
You and the other pagans
Audible as you chant next door?
Chances are, the preacher reasons,
You'll be more willing to listen
Now that your city has fallen from what it was,
More willing at least to acknowledge
Questions you haven't answered
Among the questions worth your time.

Thanksgiving Letter from Harry

I guess I have to begin by admitting
I'm thankful today I don't live in a country
My country has chosen to liberate,
That Bridgeport's my home, not Baghdad.
Thankful my chances are good, when I leave
For the Stop & Shop, that I'll be returning.
And I'm thankful my TV set is still broken.
No point in wasting energy feeling shame
For the havoc inflicted on others in my name
When I need all the strength I can muster
To teach my eighth-grade class in the low-rent district.
There, at least, I don't feel powerless.
There my choices make some difference.

This month I'd like to believe I've widened
My students' choice of vocation, though the odds
My history lessons on working the land
Will inspire any of them to farm
Are almost as small as the odds
One will become a monk or nun
Trained in the Buddhist practice
We studied last month in the unit on India.
The point is to get them suspecting the world
They know firsthand isn't the only world.

As for the calling of soldier, if it comes up in class,
It's not because I feel obliged to include it,
As you, as a writer, may feel obliged.
A student may happen to introduce it,
As a girl did yesterday when she read her essay

About her older brother, Ramon,
Listed as "missing in action" three years ago,
And about her dad, who won't agree with her mom
And the social worker on how small the odds are
That Ramon's alive, a prisoner in the mountains.

I didn't allow the discussion that followed
More time than I allowed for the other essays.
And I wouldn't take sides: not with the group
That thought the father, having grieved enough,
Ought to move on to the life still left him;
Not with the group that was glad he hadn't made do
With the next-to-nothing the world's provided,
That instead he's invested his trust in a story
That saves the world from shameful failure.

Let me know of any recent attempts on your part
To save our fellow citizens from themselves.
In the meantime, if you want to borrow Ramon
For a narrative of your own, remember that any scene
Where he appears under guard in a mountain village
Should be confined to the realm of longing. There
His captors may leave him when they move on.
There his wounds may be healed,
His health restored. A total recovery
Except for a lingering fog of forgetfulness
A father dreams he can burn away.

The Will to Power

Among the many who find the path they've chosen
Blocked by rock slides, one may resolve
To think of himself as a god,
A god with his own mysterious reasons
For providing himself with obstacles.

Among the crowd of losing candidates,
One may consider only himself responsible,
Though no one can claim he shirked the day-long
Dusty bus rides into the boondocks.
No one denies his being outspent
Twenty to one by the man who won.

To be a god among many losers
He turns away from the solace of friends
And walks to the park and rents a rowboat
And rows out into the dying lake
That might, he tells himself,
Still be teeming with life if only
He'd given more speeches on acid rain.

Then, for the hour or so he can bear it,
He's a god in earnest, though maybe a god
With a stitch in his side as he rows
Back to the boathouse, with knees
That ache a little as he walks to his bungalow.
A god who wonders what he was thinking
When he directed himself to grow old.

Maybe he wanted the chance to prove
His body's decline couldn't cow his spirit.
Maybe he wanted to test his resolve
Not to accept an offer of life everlasting
If it meant leaving his body behind.

"No," a god declares without flinching,
"That's not my style, to drop a companion,
Loyal to me from first to last."

Trash Fire

Though she's one of our friendly foursome
At this patio table, behind the roadside restaurant,
She doesn't expect us to leave our chairs
As she does when we happen to notice,
At the edge of the parking area,
The black plume of a trash fire.
Likewise, we don't expect her to stay in hers,
Given her special concern with protecting the atmosphere
From further insult, but to go and investigate.
And instead of letting ourselves feel abandoned,
We continue the conversation without her,
Sharing impressions of our travels last summer
South of Paris, through villages near the Rhône.
And when she finally returns to the patio,
She doesn't expect us to rise and follow
As she skirts the tables and enters the restaurant.
Good luck to her as she tries to persuade the owner
He ought to consider how quickly a few fires
No bigger than his add up to something serious,
A serious strain on the air. While she's gone
We use our sociable talents to fall into talk
With the elderly couple at the table beside ours,
Who've asked the waitress about the menu
In an accent we recognize. Soon we're sharing
Our memories of Quebec in a French
Whose good intentions seem to outweigh
Our shaky grammar and quaint syntax.
And that's what we're doing still
When she returns, rebuffed, to the patio.
Here we are, she can tell from a distance,

Doing our best to widen our circle
Of temporary connections. Loneliness,
Is it something she might have avoided
By choosing her friends more carefully,
Or simply a feature of what it means
To be her, she must be wondering, as she stands
Outside the circle, looking now at us
And now at the long black plume
That's turning the bright sky hazy.

Evening in the Berkshires

Maybe we have all we asked for, and this feeling
Of incompleteness as we stand by ourselves
On the patio of the hillside hotel, in twilight,
Is merely the ghostly residue of the restless,
Unappeasable, ravening will that Schopenhauer
Wrongly identifies as our essence.
Maybe all that's needed is to see the hills
Now stretching away in the late light
As a painter would, one who doesn't intend
To make use of them as a screen for his own
Regrets or longings, but to do them justice.
He isn't waiting for change. He isn't straining
To see if someone's approaching along the path
From the woods to the sloping lawn
With news that will make a difference.
He's simply intent on watching the twilight
As it settles across the valley, on noting
The details of its advent, on taking it in.
For us to wonder how long an apprenticeship
Is required before we can see as he does
Is a sign of how dependent we still feel
On masters and fellow students, on time
To provide us with years of practice.
But all that's missing may be the conviction
That what the twilight appears to be offering
Without conditions can be enjoyed as much
By those who have just arrived as by the early.
A hopeful truth if we can grasp it
Completely before the bell announces
Supper is served, and we all go in.

A Visit to West Point

Butterflies in dark caves, dervishes in the desert—
It's easier to believe in them now that I'm witnessing,
Here in a fortress classroom, English majors in uniform
Giving their full attention to Cadet Fuscaro
As he offers a PowerPoint presentation
On stream of consciousness in Virginia Woolf.

English majors soon to be off to classes
On protecting supply lines and surprising the enemy
Are struggling for a moment with the question how much
Woolf was changed by allowing the shifting moods
Of her characters to circulate through her,
The standard maneuver of thought, its bold advance
To attack a problem, suspended.

Will a class like this one inspire Cadet Fuscaro,
Stationed one day far from the Hudson,
To let his imagination flow into hostile towns
And feel what the sister of a militia member feels
When she wonders how a war will help her people?
Not likely, but not impossible,

Especially if this summer, home for vacation,
He tries his hand at a novel that goes
Where it wants to go, without a mission.
A young hero whose future looks unpredictable
Seems to me a likely beginning,
A boy whose need for loyalty to his deep convictions
Is balanced by his need to be unconvinced
Now and then, and lonely.

His father could be an army captain
Keen on the beauty of sacrifice
For the general welfare, while his mother
Might urge her son to follow through
On his interest in acting, to enroll in courses
Where he'll learn to lose himself in the parts assigned him,
King or misfit, whistle-blower or villain.

Don't be afraid, Cadet Fuscaro, to let the boy,
After finishing college, put off the choice of career—
Which you seem to have made for yourself already—
For some years of drifting. And if, in the end,
His favorite uncle nudges him toward the law,
Let him delay deciding whether to join the war
Of the D.A.'s office against the lawless or to help
The Public Defender open cases long closed.

It's your novel, Cadet Fuscaro, not mine,
But I hope you don't mind a few suggestions.
If the plot moves toward a courtroom, consider
Letting it move away soon afterward.
How far would you like your hero to stand
From the flow of talk in a restaurant
As the friend of a murdered man explains how little
Convicting the guilty has meant to her?

And in a scene at the hero's house,
Do his guests, the wrongly convicted,
Newly released from prison, listen to him
When he asks what they'd change first, if they could,

About the world he works in? And if they answer,
Can he hear them over the sound of his wondering
Who they might be if they'd been luckier,
Those unknown others they won't be now?

Not a God

If being a god implies believing yourself
Worthy of adoration from anyone
Who turns to you when others fail,
Then Larry Fenster, owner of Fenster's Bike Repair,
Isn't a god, though his customers
Swear by his skill and industry
And are eager to recommend him.

A single compliment is enough
To make Larry uneasy.
He's one of the meek, one who believes
His kind isn't likely to inherit the earth
And isn't upset about it, having considered
The sad condition the earth is in
After long neglect, the pocking and rusting.

Even harder for Larry than being praised
Would be the petitions that gods receive
And fail to answer. They can't be bothered, it seems,
No matter how great the need, or answer vaguely,
According to principles more mysterious
Than any that Larry would want to work by.

If he were a god, he wouldn't be so upset
When a bicycle race he's helped to sponsor
Isn't won by the racer who's practiced
The longest and hardest, on the roughest terrain,
Who's listened to all the tips his coach has offered
And put them to use with a faith in their power

That Larry believes would level mountains
If faith made up for a lack of talent.

When his favorite loses, it's easy to see
Larry isn't a god. Instead of blaming the loss
On some obscure infraction, he gently suggests
That instead of racing, the loser should think of his bike
As a means to explore the countryside over byroads
The racers miss out on as they streak by.
Take this map. Take this kit for testing
Whether the water's drinkable at a stream
Whose beauty we'll have no way of knowing
Unless you describe it for us when you get back.

Among the Generous

Now and then I can number myself
Among the generous, when a generous thought
Is all that's required, not action.

Now and then I'm willing to ask
If those at the front of the line at the picnic
Who pile three sandwiches on their plates,
Leaving those at the end with crackers and radishes,
May be merely provincial, not selfish.
Maybe they were exposed in school
Only to the philosophy that begins and ends
With the "I," the "I" as it muses alone
With the windows shut and the curtains drawn,
That regards the rest of the world as gossamer
Spun out by the mind for a little company.
The antidote may be simply a course or two
In other cultures, in their laws and creeds,
Their exports, fashions, and pastimes.

Now and then I can believe that the cousin
Who didn't show up on the day he promised
Meant to help me clean my flooded basement,
That he lay down after lunch, as he claims, to rest
For just ten minutes, not to sleep till sundown.
What if he isn't lazy, if his nap is akin
To the doze of a moose or bear at the zoo
As it dreams of woods and grassland,
Of drinking at dawn from a native stream.
He too could be longing for home
Even if he was born and raised here

Just as I was. But where I was right
To turn from the call of the vague and distant,
He's right, given his talents, to dream of wandering.

Now and then I'm able to wish that the friend
Who's put me third on her list of favorites
Can accept the gust of loneliness she sometimes feels
Sweeping over the breakfast table she shares
With the man she's chosen, that she can read it
As having little to do with him.
It may be merely a matter of the drizzle outside
And the muddy yard, which may call to mind
A similar morning twenty years back
In a city where she knew no one.
Now and then on my better days
I can hope she doesn't regret her choice,
That she thinks of her sadness as a gesture of sympathy
For the younger woman who will always live alone
Inside her, in a dark, one-room apartment, oblivious
To the happier woman that she's become.

Near Dusk

This is the famous witching hour
When the sun, too low to be seen,
Strikes the houses and trees,
The parked cars and pedestrians,
Head on, if it strikes them at all,
Bathing them in an umber glow
That every connoisseur of light
Would be out in the street enjoying
If the hour didn't happen to be congenial
To shadows as well. Notice how tall
They've grown, those that at noon
Were thickset midget mascots
Trotting along beside us strollers
Just to keep up. Now to keep up
We're the ones who must do the trotting.
And notice how thin they've grown,
As if hollowed by disappointment,
By having to live out their lives in exile.

Light from the side, an umber glow
Implying to students of fine impressions
The moment is not a portal
To a life beyond it, that what is
Is enough if seen with a mind
Free of the dogma of expectations.
And shadows that lean away.
How restless they are, how sorry
To live among us, the satisfied.
How much better if they could go back
To the homeland they fought for and lost,
If only to fight and lose again.

A Teacher Looks Back

If I'd had a choice, I'd have secured a place
Among those in the highest order, the great hearts,
Who teach for the joy of passing their joy along,
As someone who loves the water
Won't rest till a friend afraid of the water
Learns to love swimming beyond the shallows;
The enthusiasts who forget to stop with the bell,
Who love to repeat themselves after school
For the slow learners, never turning away to notice
It's growing dark outside and about to rain.

Because I always turned, I'd have aligned myself
With the dutiful teachers one level down
Had my sense of duty proved strong enough.
Still, I admired them from a distance,
Those who had hoped to get home before dark
But stayed to be true to their principles.
The wind dies, the sails hang slack on the packet boat
While down below the engine starts up, grinding
And grunting its way to the dock where the passengers
Are greeted by those assigned to greet them.

With my will, like my heart, too feeble,
I had to fall back on my fear of vanishing
Without a speck of proof that I ever lived here.
Teach well, I told myself, and maybe a few
Long after I'd gone would call me to mind
When they remembered their progress from cave
To sunny harbor crowded with sails.
A few might want to take my image on board,

It pleased me to hope, though I wasn't blind
To how thin their hulls were, how leaky.
Better their bobbing boats, I decided,
Than a landscape indifferent to my departure,
Not one shade darker or more pale.

The False and the True

The story she told at their first meeting,
Last spring in the health food store,
That she'd just returned from a year at a school
For Buddhist nuns outside Benares,
Turned out to be false, the jade barrette
That loosely gathered her waist-length hair
Made in Detroit. But his feelings for her
Revealed the partial truth behind them:
That she'd dreamed of going, and would have,
If she'd been able to save enough for plane fare
And didn't have a daughter in high school
Here in Erie County and a job at the hospital.

As for his tacit hint that his quiet demeanor
Was a sign of a peace-loving character, that was true,
She later discovered, though his conversion to peace
Happened more recently than he'd suggested.
Just a month before, in fact, when his doctor warned him
His ulcer was worse, and no wonder,
What with his years of quarreling with his colleagues
In County Health. But who can blame him,
She wants to know, for his outrage
At their lax enforcement of pollution laws?

It's true she still hasn't told him about her brush
With cancer last fall. True he's been silent
About the operation scheduled for spring
To repair a heart valve. But if their silence
Has cast a shadow between them,
Each knows the other knows that the odds are slim

They'll have more than a score of years together.
Meanwhile, here they are,
With time enough to list the efforts they'll make,
If given a chance, for the other's sake,
Many of them ambitious and meant sincerely.

In the Park

How willing to wait they are, this young mother
And father standing at the foot of the small slide
As if they loved nothing better than watching their boy
Hesitate at the top, and would be happy
To stand there till dark without once suggesting

It's time for action. They can't be sure he'll remember
One detail from this scene, but even if he forgets,
They could be thinking, their refusal to urge him on
May keep working beneath the surface,
Nursing the growth of confidence in a voice within

That will help their boy, naturally tentative,
To push forward at his own tempo. For a gain like that
Their waiting appears a trifling price to pay,
Though they realize that the trust they're promoting
May one day inspire their son to travel far

On a private mission, too far for them to visit.
Now and then a card without a return address
May suggest to them he hasn't much company
But his pen and notebook, and the words
That willingly give themselves to his service,

And the words he has to go looking for,
The ones he finds abused on the street
And tries to shepherd home to his study,
Away from street gangs and lives of crime.
May he be happy as he soaps them down

And dries them, and dresses them in apparel
That befits their differences. May his hope prove true,
When he gives them parts in the script he's drafting,
That they speak with feeling and that what they feel
Suits them for life in a decent family.

At Darwin's House

Though I'd like to believe that the future
Holds more possibility than the past,
I have some trouble with speculations like Darwin's
In his later years that the social virtues
May be still evolving, that one fine day
People may find it natural to be civil.

No sign so far that selection and variation,
Those engines that eased us away
From the other primates, will ease us along
Till the envy stirred up in Joseph's brothers
By their father's favorite will seem strange,
Far stranger, at least, than it does today.

As for good examples, the past can offer many.
The Darwins themselves might be the equal
Of the best families the future holds.
It's hard to imagine siblings to come
Who will play together in greater harmony
Than the children of Charles and Emma,
Brought up in a spacious country house
On the Kentish uplands.

I wouldn't hesitate to be one of them,
If required to be born again in another family,
Though it's true I'd be one of ten, ten children
Sharing the love of two parents.
But our father would work at home,
Not in London, and the help of servants

Would free our mother to listen attentively
Whenever we felt the need to confide.

As for molding our characters,
Our parents would try to teach by example.
Mother's lending library for the village children
Would make a deep impression,
Like Father's courtesy to his employees,
How he raised his voice to the gardener
Only once, for mistreating an underling.

And they'd agree to suspend the rule
Common in other country houses
That restricted play to the nursery.
Fine with them if the parlor sofas
Suffer our jumping and butting,
If the chairs are moved for a game of railroad.

They'd disagree only on matters less practical,
Like whether Scripture is divine or human.
Mother would worry that Father's doubts
Would keep him from living with her in the afterworld.
Father's investigations would leave him resigned
To a nature that cares for the aggregate only,
Not the individual. The contrast
Might lead us children to feel at home
As much with contradiction as with consensus.

No progress in family happiness,
Just in the number of families as happy

As Darwin's was. Just more children provided
With the privileges his children enjoyed
Along with a lower death rate, not the one in ten
Who never became adults in his England.

How would it differ, a family more civil
Than Darwin's was? Will parents to come
Grieve a loss more deeply or purely
Than the parents of Annie Darwin did
When she died at the age of ten?
Will they grow more quiet when asked if their joys
Outweigh their sorrows, or hesitate longer
Before they try to answer in the affirmative?

The God of Dogs

Billions of years had to pass before the concern
And vigilance of the god of dogs
Made themselves manifest, and a wet mutt
Could sleep by the stove while a winter wind
Banged the shutters. So many eons of preparation
Before our planet cooled and crusted.
So long a stretch before the first clouds opened
To moisten the burning marl, the first rain
Slowly filling the low spots to make an ocean
Or shallow inlet or landlocked pool
Where the earliest speck of life was warmed into being.
And then the teeming waters and the pioneer species
Edging up on the sand so their descendents could serve
As the earliest ancestors of dogs and humans.
The day a dog pack and band of hunters
Ventured to share their gifts—dog nose, man spear—
Marked a big step in the plan of the god of dogs,
Like the winter night a dog first edged into camp
And found it cozier than the woods because the dog god
Had done his groundwork, first endowing humans
With the wit to construct a lean-to and build a fire.
And then the snug tepee, sod house, log house,
Clapboard A-frame plastered against the drafts.
By the time the village became a city
Too far from the woods for hunting, the god of dogs
Had spiked the human gene pool with an extra
Tincture of loneliness so that even a dog
Asleep by the stove provided some company
On blustery nights when the dark felt menacing.
And to keep the master from infecting his dog

With human fears, the farsighted god of dogs
Provided him with the gift of self-distraction.
It's time to clean the attic again.
It's time to cull the shelves, removing the books
He hasn't opened in years to make room for new ones.
By then the sun's up and the dog's awake,
Eager for a frisk in the park and the sudden
Concert of odors that welcomes its kind
Into a paradise that would make its master jealous
If the god of dogs hadn't thought to provide him
With a knack for metaphor. "This literal park,"
The master reasons, "might well betoken
A park of the spirit that waits to receive me."
And then he muses about its whereabouts,
Losing himself in the kind of cloudy question
That allows the dog time to sniff in the bushes
Or tree a squirrel. And then, if needed, the question
If he'll know his paradise when he finds it,
Or only later, looking back.

To My Body

If I've read your silence correctly,
You've never been sullen,
Never resentful I've treated you more
As a master treats a servant
Than as friend treats friend.

On the dark day when you'll be too weak
To obey my wishes, I don't imagine you
Feeling relieved, glad to be free
Of a partner who failed to understand you.
I suspect you'll be troubled,
Knowing how lost I'll be without you.

I know how lucky I am
That you've been so patient,
So willing to sit for hours—
Now that your shoulder has almost healed
And the pain in your back has responded to therapy—
Without complaining, motionless
Except for the hand holding the pen.

What can I do, I wonder, while you still
Can bestir yourself for my sake, to show you
I'm not ungrateful. Shall we take off a day
Together soon? Shall we stroll the streets
Or hike in the mountains?

It's up to you, if you choose the mountains,
Whether we climb to test your limits of breath

And muscle, and embrace exhaustion,
Or linger in a thicket of nuts and berries.

And if we linger, it's your choice whether we eat,
There and then, all that we gather,
As if that meal would be our last one,
Or save a portion so that tomorrow
Won't seem ungenerous,
If not so generous as today.

A Sect

More jubilant by far than many Christians
On the birthday of Jesus, the many pagans
Crowding into the square this New Year's Eve,
Though by now they must realize that the baby
Whose birth they're about to witness
Is doomed to grow old and die in a year,
Just as the last one did, and the one before,
Without a crumb of hope in a second coming.
How explain their singing and shouting
On a night so cold they're dancing in place?
Some, no doubt, have persuaded themselves
This is the year when the boat they've been steering
Through choppy seas enters a harbor
They've glimpsed before only in dreams,
The year when their lives begin in earnest.
But others among them must have an inkling
The sea isn't a test they can pass
To graduate into something else.
Sooner or later, they have to figure,
It will swallow them up with all they cherish
In a year no different from this one,
The one they're now ardently welcoming.
Why would they want to collaborate
With the enemy, to cozy up to a power
No tactics of theirs will slow by a minute?
If they want to contend, in the face of experience,
That the music they're dancing to
Has been beamed from afar with the news
That the passing away of years is an illusion,
How do they handle the fact that a witness

Looking on attentively from the sidelines
Can't find the frequency on his own equipment?
Chances are this isn't the first time
He's stood in the cold on the last night of the year
And wondered just what it is he might be missing,
What it might sound like to those who hear.

To Happiness

If you're not approaching, I hope at least
You're off to comfort someone who needs you more,
Not lost or wandering aimlessly
Or drawn to the shelter of well-lit rooms
Where people assume you've arrived already.

If you're coming this way, send me the details—
The name of the ship, the port it leaves from—
So I can be down on the dock to help you
Unload your valises, your trunks and boxes,
And stow them in the big van I'll have rented.

I'd like this to be no weekend stay
Where a single change of clothes is sufficient.
Bring clothes for all seasons, enough to fill a closet;
And instead of a single book for the bedside table
Bring boxes of all your favorites.

I'll be eager to clear half my shelves to make room,
Eager to read any titles you recommend.
If we've many in common, feel free to suggest
They prove my disposition isn't to blame
For your long absence, just some problems of attitude,

A few bad habits you'll help me set to one side.
We can start at dinner, which you're welcome
To cook for us while I sweep and straighten
And set the table. Then light the candles
You've brought from afar for the occasion.

Light them and fill the room I supposed I knew
With a glow that shows me I was mistaken.
Then help me decide if I'm still the person I was
Or someone else, someone who always believed in you
And imagined no good reasons for your delay.

Remorse

Now I'm sorry I used my authority as host
To hold the talk last night at dinner
Fixed on the subject of global warming,
On the lasting injury done to the planet
By the chimneys of our country
And our exhaust pipes.

Now I regret the injury done to freedom
By my assuming one topic
Trumped all the others, that mine
Was the capital of the evening while others
Were only provincial villages offering tribute.

Then too the wound that Nancy suffered
When I labeled her wish to speak of the mulch
Doing her roses a world of good
A mere evasion, a pathetic attempt
To deny the disaster of the energy bill
Now being hustled by oil money through Congress.

Tired of my tirade, the guests left early.
They'd hoped to participate in a play of thought
That discovered its plot as it proceeded,
Not to sit in the audience with a notebook
While I led them step by step down a path
They could see the end of from miles off.

I should have tried to calm myself by supposing
The planet may not be as doomed
As it seems to be. But if it is,

And tomorrow's the day it ends,
Nancy will still choose to go out
In the morning with her hoe and clippers.

She'll still want to declare her faith
That the gardener's calling
Is one of the age-old human practices
That might have done more to help us
If nurtured more often by conversation,
The open variety that allows each subject
The margin it needs to sprout and flower.

Unfading Pages

Whatever good my aunt did, she did for the sake
Of the good itself, not for a heavenly payoff.
But she might have accepted, if offered, a heavenly witness,
An angelic scribe getting what matters down on a page
Not exposed to flood or fire, dry rot or weevils.

Then she could have avoided grieving so much
Over losing Grandpa's diary in the move
From her ample house to her small apartment.
No small comfort, the thought of another copy
Safe in a reading room, ready for scholar-angels

Concerned with creatures much like themselves
Though sadly mortal. A few might be specialists
In the sheer persistence of Lithuanian immigrants
Arriving, like Grandpa, on a freighter from Bremen,
Determined to stay, whatever happened.

Safe, too, in a book so inclusive,
A copy of the letter an editor took the time
To write me forty years ago, however frazzled
He may have been, when returning a group of poems.
Three full pages about mannered diction

And runaway metaphor that I learned a lot from.
Here I've misplaced it, along with the name
Of the writer and the magazine, but there
It's brought from the stacks to an angel
Intrigued by examples of exertion on earth

Beyond the confines of common duty.
And in situations without original documents,
The scribe would consult reports of angelic eyewitnesses
So nothing of value would be lost to oblivion.
How grand a gift, the consolation a book like that

Could offer my neighbor about her son,
Dead already four long years from leukemia,
Now that the words and gestures of the boy's
Lone decade have begun to fade. How helpful
To know that a scribe committed to truth

Had made room for them in his annals,
That the pages would likely be studied one day
By an angel moved by the boy's singularity
And not inclined to argue that he was needed
Elsewhere more than he was at home.

Birthday

Now that the time remaining is insubstantial,
I need to review my history while asking
What exactly it suggests I've lived for,
What pleasures or duties, what moods
Of brief elation or extended calm.

To expect a meaning deeper than that,
To believe in a purpose beyond my own
Furthered by me all along without my knowing,
Is to warm myself at a fire painted on canvas.

If I want the company of the nonexistent,
I'm better off with the crowd of shadows who lost
Their only chance to escape the darkness
On the night I happened to be conceived.

I wonder how many of them would have felt more lucky
With the family allotted me than I did, more pleased
With the neighborhood. So many chances for them
To go out and investigate, in streets that often bored me,
Rumors that the beautiful had been sighted locally.

The sassafras tree in the lot behind the shoe store
Might have been mentioned by some,
Or the straight-backed, white-haired woman
Waiting for the bus in the rain at Main and Biddle.

Even the bowl of cherries she left in her kitchen
Is worth their regard, a bowl they might have painted
In a rush of sympathy for objects small and frail,

Insubstantial and insignificant, or a rush of awe
At how ready the cherries and the bowl appear
To give themselves to the light that's left them,
With nothing held in reserve for a better day.

Highland Street

Though our neighbor wasn't a friend of ours,
We feel friendly enough to her memory
To adjust our schedules on the day of her funeral.
And if her thoughts on the street we shared
Are unknown to us, how Highland
Changed for her over forty years,
We're willing to raise the question
At least for the hour it takes us
To drive to the cemetery and back.

And if the absence we feel as we turn
Down Highland Street and park in the driveway
Isn't the same as grief, it still may tell us
Something about who she was,
About the particular tune
She played on the keyboard of Highland Street
Among the many she might have played.

Only her friends can say for certain
How the street looked different to her
After her stroke, when she had to use a walker
To do her shopping or visit the library.
But that shouldn't keep us from wondering
If it felt less welcoming or less solid,
An open street suddenly locked away,
A confident, stalwart street
Suddenly frail and filmy.

Do you think she was only joking
When she told us her favorite city was Florence,

A city we knew she had never visited?
And how do you read the bright red dress
She came to prefer? As a token of joy
Still known to her on her better days,
Or as a tactic to prevail on joy
To find a place for Highland Street
On its busy schedule, to make a side trip
If it wasn't working too far away?

Grass

Not much evidence, on a walk through town,
That the god in whose image we've been created
Is passionate about justice, not when compared
To the evidence of his love for grass.
Just look at the these lawns,
How cared for they are, how cherished,
The meager ones as well as the grand.

Maybe the planet was once all grass,
A grass-bound weekend retreat for a god
Who refreshed himself, after weekday duties,
With leisurely walks over springy greensward,
With mowing, edging, and watering,
Like any grass-lover in the neighborhood.

A planet all for himself at first, though later,
After his schedule at work became so crowded
That he rarely managed to get away,
He thought of adding fauna to keep the blades
From growing so thick they choked themselves.
Hence the drilling and nibbling insects,
Hence the chomping and browsing quadrupeds.

And when the crowds of grass-eaters grew so great
That the fields were overgrazed, the roots endangered,
He had to create some eaters of meat as well.
And when the carnivores threatened to thin the flocks
To nothing, he thought us up, us hunters and herders
With a passion for grass the equal of his.

That was the plan, though he must have been vexed
By the struggles for land that soon followed.
He must have been hurt when the landless clustered in cities
And later when cities gradually muscled outward
With brick and blacktop into glade and meadow.
What a shock for him when he found,
At the edge of the woods, his favorite trail
Blocked by the parking lot of another church
Built in his honor, another mosque or synagogue.

It shouldn't be any surprise that his visits
Ceased long ago, that now when he gives a report
To the gods of other realms met in assembly,
He lists our planet as one of the few
Failed experiments in his dominions.

Your mistake, says one of the other delegates,
Was supposing a god could do his job
Responsibly in a five-day work week.
Your mistake, says another, was thinking yourself
So needed at work that you skimped on the pleasure
Of witnessing how the grass was getting on.

To Duty

You ask me to shun deception, to embrace the truth
Even when it comes as a gust of wind
To snuff out a final flicker of hope. And yet
You also require my acting as if I'm concerned
With the welfare of those I'm indifferent to.

You claim to be a friend, but no other friend
As ready to give advice as you are
Seems so careless about my pleasure.
None assumes without question, as you do,
That the hardest choice must be the right one.

Do you see yourself as an agent for someone far off
Who regards me as an instrument, not as an end?
Do I have to remind you how badly you can go wrong
When you're too proud to share authority
With the voice of common feelings?

If I were you, I'd be glad that your rule
Obliging me to visit old Aunt Maria
Is backed by the pleasure I take in her company,
In hearing more stories about my parents
As I sample a slice of her delicate crumb cake.

And in harder cases, I fall back on the pleasure
Of deciding I'm someone who can't be happy
Devoting himself to the gratification of whim.
And then the artist's pleasure, which to you means nothing,
Of getting my part down, of acting

So much like someone happy to be of service,
I forget I'm acting. No need for me then to ride
Shut in your car. I can take to my bike
And coast along on my own, the sun
Warm on my shoulders, wind in my hair.

Report from Eden

Though the gardens here turn out to be nothing
To write home about, the weedy side lots
Prove the perfect habitat for cicadas, whose trilling
Is taken to be authentic native music.
It's one of the local pleasures to mark the difference
Between the hum that calls for a mate
And the churr that implies, "This is my twig,
Don't crowd me," and to tell these two
From a click whose meaning is still under study.
The people here don't need to believe
The concert's for them before they listen
As hard as they can on their evening stroll
After a day in the bottling plant, shoe store, or smithy.
And they don't believe their stroll will take them
To an elsewhere that's more amenable to their wishes.
They're rambling under arching branches along a street
Where many people before them have rambled
Feeling equally lucky to enjoy the privilege.
The neighbor who seems to be playing the same piece
On her upright piano whenever they happen past
Isn't practicing to be perfect. She's doing her part
To usher the day out in a style that's fitting,
Inspired by the cicadas as they squeak and cheep
From the dewy grass of the status quo.
Even the lovers here seem free of longing.
They don't believe tomorrow will bring them anything
They don't possess this evening, though they love to sing
"If I had a nickel I'd give it to you," pretending they need
To turn from the limited funds of the indicative
To the endless bounty of the subjunctive.

As for what tomorrow is planning to take away,
To them it seems only fitting that other lovers
Now waiting in line to be born
Will be granted the run of the streets one day,
With a chance to listen while the descendents
Of these cicadas run through their repertoire.
That's why a visitor here is likely
To resist the temptation to stay, because the natives
Endorse the obliteration that may feel to him
Like a calamity, a case of gross injustice
That in an Eden more friendly could be appealed.

On the Bus to Pittsburgh

Ordinarily, I wouldn't bother a stranger
I met on a bus with my plan
For saving the country. But you
Seem like a person ready to listen.
I take those brochures you've been studying
About walks through Wales and Scotland
To mean you're eager to leave this country
Whenever you can, that you've concluded,
As I once did, that change is impossible
Here where the people seem to enjoy believing
The lies their leaders enjoy concocting.
But may I suggest you're ignoring
Evidence like our jury system,
Whose basic reliability proves we still care,
Now and then, about justice?
That's where my plan comes in,
Which begins with putting our voting machines
In storage and choosing our leaders
As we do our juries, by lottery.

Are you with me so far, or does your silence
Mean you don't believe I'm a practical person?
Try suspending your doubts for a while
And asking yourself how you might feel
If at the next stop an official got on
To announce that we aren't headed to Pittsburgh
As scheduled, that the luck of the lottery
Has chosen our group for Washington.
Of course, we'd cry out in protest
At the thought of the wounds

That four years away from home
Would inflict on our schedules.
But wouldn't our outrage be evidence
We were free of the lust for power
That now contaminates most contenders?

I hope I'm right in supposing your looking around
Doesn't mean you're thinking of changing seats,
Just that you're wondering, as I am,
If our fellow riders show any obvious sign
Of potential for pubic service. What's your opinion
Of that thin young woman four rows ahead
Adjusting her makeup in her compact mirror
As if to charm her way through the world?
Do you think she can scold a Cabinet
Into consensus? The odds she'll try
Don't seem to me any worse than the odds
Those noisy poker players behind us
Will decide it's time to forgo bluffing and posturing.
As for the old woman behind the driver,
Don't you agree that her dowdy,
Flowery hat might be a sign of a confident
Disregard for the crowd's opinion
That could offer a new regime some integrity?

In a minute I'll let you get back to your reading,
I promise. The brochure with the cover photo
Of Hadrian's Wall looks interesting. Also the one
Showing a tent pitched by a dark-age ruin.
But if ruins are what attract you,

You don't have to go abroad.
Plenty of chances here for a busload
Of leaders-to-be to feel like travelers
Musing among the stumps of toppled columns
Strewing a Forum, travelers with the job
Of deciding which temples to rebuild first thing.

For me, of course, it all goes back to the question
Which gods might be willing to accept our lottery
As a call for help. And then the question what steps
Would we like them to sponsor first
So our path leads us to voting booths
Lit better than the booths we're used to,
Those closet caves, those dungeons.

At the Oak Street Restaurant

If I hadn't promised to second the speech
A friend is giving tonight at the Preservation Society
About the house, derelict now for a decade,
On Franklin Street, I'd linger over dessert,
Prolonging the pleasure I take in admiring
The woman alone at the window table
Who's been filling a notebook steadily for an hour.
To me she's remarkable, her total withdrawal
From her surroundings—the other diners,
The river outside the window,
The traffic over the bridge, the park beyond.
Remarkable, though I might not remark her
If she didn't appeal to me for other reasons. Slender,
A little angular, dark hair, midthirties at most,
Still young from my perspective, though maybe from hers
Her life is half gone. Time for her to make a list
Of all she hopes to do in the half still left her.
In the smaller fraction left me, watching her write
Seems to be one of my deeper preferences,
Along with helping to bring houses of interest
Back to their glory days when the earliest owners
Bustled among the living. It's my gift to the dead,
To show them that details of their own devising
Still give pleasure. As for the not-yet-born,
Could be this woman is drafting a story
That will leave them more wakeful,
More aware of alternatives to the path
They may have identified with necessity.
I wonder if the friend she'll show it to first
Will read it as carefully as I would.

The thought that he might, I have to admit,
Troubles me more than I'd like it to.
She'd be grateful, I'm sure, for any pointers,
Her commitment to writing well
Stronger by far than her fear
Of being critiqued without sympathy.
Hence her concentration; hence her resistance
To the casual facts around her, the accidental.
As for me, I'm trying to make the most of the accident
Of her happening to enter this very restaurant
As I sat alone at my table
Going over my notes for my talk tonight.
Though I'm sorry we haven't met, I don't regret,
As I glance at my watch and pull my coat on,
That I set my notes aside to focus on her. So what
If my transitions tonight are a little raggedy,
My pauses a little too long and frequent,
As I help my friend explain why the house on Franklin
Deserves to shine as it did before.

The Triumph of Time

Maybe soon a boatload of images
Sailing into port from the long-lost world
Of our time together
Won't have to be quarantined.

Maybe soon I won't be afraid of an outbreak
Of wild remorse. I'll be down on the dock
Calmly inspecting the cargo
As if it belonged to someone else.

I'll be free to wonder
What happened to you
After you sailed away
From our reefs and squalls.

I won't need to think of you then
As condemned by restlessness
To grow tired of every haven
You first find welcoming.

Then I'll be able to imagine you
Walking to work on a blustery
Winter morning free of regret
That you didn't select a kinder climate.

Then I'll hope you interpret
The glitter of trees crusted with snow,
And the small brown wedges of sparrows
Distinct in the branches,

As evidence that the street,
Even before you hear the cheeping
And glimpse the fluttering,
Isn't as empty as it appears.

Talk

Now we're too old to waste even one
Of the weekly dinners still left us
As we wasted the last one,
With talk about reputation:
Which names have been hustled away
By agents known and unknown
From the high table of fashion,
Which new ones propped in the vacant chairs.

In any novel we'd deem worth reading,
A topic like that would be assigned
To minor characters only,
While the few we're most concerned with,
Finding the dining room in the fancy hotel
Too still and stuffy,
Would be out on the porch by themselves,
Engaged with one of the larger questions.

Here are Pierre and Prince Andrew
Lost in their dialogue about life,
Whether it may be said to have a purpose.
Though one says yes, and the other no,
And neither's impressed by the other's arguments,
They aren't tempted to give up trying.

And though we know, like gods, how soon
Events will lead them to change their answers,
We still don't want to shorten their talk
By a single sentence, knowing as well

How few exchanges are left them
As full as this one, as earnest.

How many are left us,
Who are twice as old as they are,
Is a question we needn't address directly.
Hovering in the background, it may work
To give the topics we choose a sharper focus.
Just so the focus isn't so sharp it keeps us
From making a detour when a detour beckons.
Just so we're free to choose, if we want, a path
Too long for us to reach the end.

To a Young Poet

However chair-bound the trade may feel,
Keep in mind how free it would likely appear
To a carpenter you tried to describe it to
As he waited in the return line at Thruway Builders.
Of the fifty boards delivered to him last week,
A dozen have proven too warped for flooring.
And where are the hinges he ordered from the catalog?

Chair-bound, but consider how free you are
Compared to a scholar of ancient Hittite
Who's had to give up her hope of finding a letter
From Uriah, the Hittite captain, to his wife, Bathsheba.
Now she must settle for fragments of royal boasts
And bills of lading, for a merchant's complaint
On a missing order of spikenard from Egypt.

As you pull your chair up to the desk,
You needn't settle for any theme
That doesn't intrigue you. And all you need to begin
Is a notebook with a dictionary open beside it,
And the will to see where your thoughts will lead you
When unconstrained by the tactics
You tend to confine them to, and the purposes.

No way to tell beforehand if the carpenter
Will play a minor or major part in your poem.
No way to tell if the scholar of Hittite
Will lament for many stanzas her choice of vocation
Or laugh at the bias toward the plots of romance

She shares with her times, and then return
To her monograph on the Hittite verb.

Only at the end will you know which of your detours
Is relevant, and even then it's useful to ask how much
Your perspective is limited by your history.
Are you one of the many masons in ancient Egypt
Proud of their work on the pyramids,
Or are you the lone one who thinks to himself,
As he saunters home with his bag of tools,
What a colossal blunder.

So many decades wasted
Making a mountain of cut stone
When, with a tenth of the outlay,
The kingdom might be enhanced
By a thousand gardens, public retreats
Where workers could stroll at their ease on feast days
As if they were born for pleasure as well as toil.

A Hundred Years

Even if the air in a hundred years
Isn't any less breathable than it is now
And the planet isn't too crowded for comfort,
We still have the problem that not one person
We know now will be alive then.

As for you and me, we'll exist, if at all,
Only as images pasted in brittle albums
Or loose in a box. In one, a middle-aged woman
In a light-colored dress and flowery hat
May stand alone by a dogwood tree.
In another, an elderly man in shirt sleeves
May lean against the patchy trunk of a sycamore.

If we can step back from our need to be recognized
And turn to the recognizing of kindred spirits,
We might enjoy the thought of two cousins to come
Taking the box down from a closet shelf
One summer evening and sifting through it
As they sit outside on the patio
While their children play nearby on the swings.

They don't know us, it's true, but we know them,
Know their pleasure in summer and summer houses
(Assuming the summers then haven't grown too sultry),
Their wish to be part of a family history,
Their regret that their elders neglected to write
On the back of each photograph

The name of the subject
With a sentence or two of biography.

Now imagine those distant cousins wondering
If the dogwood and sycamore are somehow key
To understanding our characters,
The trees that grew on the streets of our childhood
Or the ones we were most concerned with
When their biome seemed most beleaguered.

No need for us to care if our cousins
Get all the facts wrong. The truth of their history
Won't be the issue then, but their true wish
To know us better than the facts allow them,
To leap the gully between our locale and theirs.

Though sorry our love of life has been extinguished,
They'll hope it led us to many projects
They could endorse completely,
Including, for instance, writing a book
That argues children who play
On tree-lined streets tend to feel less lonely
Than those who don't, and more protected.

A lost book, to be sure, after a hundred years,
But one that a lover of trees in their era
May be inspired to write again.

MARK DELLAS

Carl Dennis is the author of nine previous works of poetry, as well as as a collection of essays, *Poetry as Persuasion*. In 2000 he received the Ruth Lilly Prize from *Poetry Magazine* and the Modern Poetry Association for his contribution to American poetry. In 2002 his book *Practical Gods* (Penguin, 2001) won the Pulitzer Prize. He lives in Buffalo, New York.